ABOUT THE AUTHOR

Bill Tidy was born in Preston in 1933, and moved to Liverpool in 1940 in time for the Blitz – which he survived. He also survived the obligatory office-boy job in a shipping office, and later a three-year stint with the army in Germany, Korea, and Japan where his first cartoon appeared in a Japanese newspaper. On leaving the army he joined a Liverpool advertising agency, and took up cartooning in 1957.

The Fosdyke Sagas have become comic classics; he has recently embarked on writing for children; and 'The Great Eric Ackroyd Disaster' was staged as a musical at the Oldham Coliseum. Bill Tidy also contributes to *Punch, Private Eye,* the *Daily Mirror*, BBC, ITV, advertising agencies, and everyone else. He received the Granada TV 'What the Papers Say' award for Cartoonist of the Year in 1974, and the Society of Strip Illustrators award in 1980.

His wife is a Neapolitan, and they have three children.

BILL TIDY'S
LITTLE RUDE BOOK

Bill Tidy drew the pictures
Graham Nown wrote the stories

NEW ENGLISH LIBRARY

A New English Library Original Publication, 1984

Copyright © 1984 by Bill Tidy/Oddfax

All rights reserved. No part of this publication may be reproduced or transmitted, in any form or by any means, without permission of the publishers.

First NEL Paperback Edition December 1984

Conditions of sale: This book is sold subject to the condition that it shall not, by way of trade or otherwise, be lent, resold, hired out, or otherwise circulated without the publisher's prior consent in any form of binding or cover other than that in which it is published and without a similar condition including this condition being imposed on the subsequent purchaser.

NEL Books are published by
New English Library,
Mill Road, Dunton Green,
Sevenoaks, Kent.
Editorial office: 47 Bedford Square, London WC1B 3DP

Photoset by Rowland Phototypesetting Ltd,
Bury St Edmunds, Suffolk

Made and printed in Great Britain by
Cox and Wyman Ltd.,
Cardiff Road, Reading

0 450 05753 4

BILL TIDY'S
LITTLE RUDE BOOK

INTRODUCTION

Few of us can resist a good bit of gossip or a spicy story – even better if it is about someone we know! Who does what to whom – and more important, how often – preoccupies a great chunk of our lives. As an obsession it's indecently below the belt. But whole industries have been launched on it and continue to flourish.

This little volume charts some of the bizarre extremes to which people push themselves for love, how sex-drive drove some round the bend and the daft things done to deserve divorce. What's more, there are some cautionary tales included. Three hundred stud rabbits dropped dead from exhaustion after chasing mates in a Barcelona heatwave – Costa Brava Romeos beware! And to those ladies with silicone extras up top: be warned that if you go flying at high altitudes, poor pressurisation could lead to mid-air explosion and embarrassing deflation.

The stories selected for inclusion in this small volume are those that particularly appealed to me and I hope that the images that they conjured up in my mind tickle your own personal fancy.

Bill Tidy
June 1984

INNOCENT ABROAD

An archbishop flew to New York and gave an airport press conference on landing. As questions were fired from all sides, one reporter barked, 'What do you think of the brothels on the East Side?' Wary of the press and anxious not to be misquoted, the archbishop cautiously replied, 'Are there any?' The lunchtime editions splashed: 'Archbishop's First Question: Are There Any Brothels on the East Side?'

BARE-FACED CHEEK

Nudes at a council art show had problems with nickers when more than twenty portraits of naked women vanished from displays at Knowsley, Merseyside, within hours of being hung.

Councillors told artists not to submit any more nudes for exhibition. 'The public couldn't keep their hands off them,' a spokesman said. 'We just could not afford a security guard next to every portrait of a naked girl.'

DOUBLE INDEMNITY

The armed robbery happened so quickly that those who saw it could remember only two things about it. Witnesses in a Turin court, asked to recall the woman who had wielded the gun, were all mesmerised by her extremely large bust.

The judge asked the lady defendant standing in the dock if she could, well, help with identification. When she obliged by unbuttoning her blouse the judge took one look and immediately released her.

JEEPERS CREEPERS

Unlike the old days when your average Peeping Tom would catch his death in damp undergrowth waiting for a glimpse through someone's curtains, a new vogue in voyeurism has emerged.

Presumably in the interests of saving time, some peepers are marching straight up to the front door and talking people into taking their clothes off.

One plausible pest went from door to door posing as a council medical officer, smooth-talking housewives into stripping off for him. He was so convincing that even when husbands arrived home unexpectedly and caught him at work, he coolly persuaded them to peel off too.

FROM RACK TO RUIN

Lindi St Clair, nickname Miss Whiplash, ran a London dungeon of love where she earned a living doing painful things to rich men. But the sex-torture queen received a nasty blow from the taxman in the shape of a £44,000 bill.

The Inland Revenue decided that she could not claim allowances for a collection of racks, gallows, manacles, mirrors and life-size blow-up dolls. Lindi complained, 'I am not being allowed a fair crack of the whip.'

At last report she was worried about being forced out of business onto the dole where she would not be optimistic about finding a job. 'Who would employ a woman who only knows how to pour hot wax over men and put them in chains for a living?' she asked.

SHOWING A CLEAN PAIR OF HEELS

Fast-footed shoe fetishist George Ronald resorted to bizarre ploys to persuade women to part with their footwear. One favourite was to stop them in the street, point out that their shoes were dirty and offer to clean them. The unwary woman barely had time to slip out her foot before Ronald was legging up the road with his booty, leaving the dazed victim to hobble home.

Another trick that always worked was to flag down a lady driver and tell her that her car was leaking oil. He would then gallantly offer to repair it – using the heel of her shoe, of course. More amazing than Ronald's antics was the fact that countless women readily agreed – only to watch him disappear in a cloud of dust with their footwear. When he was finally brought to heel he admitted getting kicks from £689 worth of stolen shoes.

THE MAN WHO WAS ALLERGIC TO WOMEN

Jim Higham had to stop looking at beautiful girls – because they made him sneeze. The mere sight of a curvy figure in a TV beauty contest or a newspaper pin-up picture was enough to make him reach for his hanky.

Even thinking about them started Jim sneezing, which did not make life easy when he caught a cold – his wife was convinced he just had one thing on his mind.

Jim, from Stowmarket, Suffolk, suffered endless embarrassment. An allergy specialist said his sneezing was an emotional reaction to the sight of beautiful women. His only advice was to stop looking at them – and save hankies.

A SMASHING NIGHT OUT

A couple thought they had found the perfect spot for a night of undisturbed passion under the stars – the roof of their local supermarket.

Their sexy romp came amiss, however, when they rolled straight through the skylight and plunged fifteen feet into the store, demolishing grocery displays and glassware and triggering all the security alarms. Police raced to the store in Stratford, London, and one officer broke his arm climbing over the debris. The embarrassed couple were unhurt, save for a gashed head, and greatly relieved when the police decided not to bring charges.

STOP, GET READY, GO!

Doctors at Glasgow Royal Infirmary devised a bra which operated like traffic lights to tell the wearer whether it was safe to have sex. It worked on the principle that a woman's temperature rises about one degree when she ovulates. The heat-sensitive bra turned red when the temperature went up and changed to green – presumably for Go – when it fell. Anyone whose partner was colour blind had serious problems.

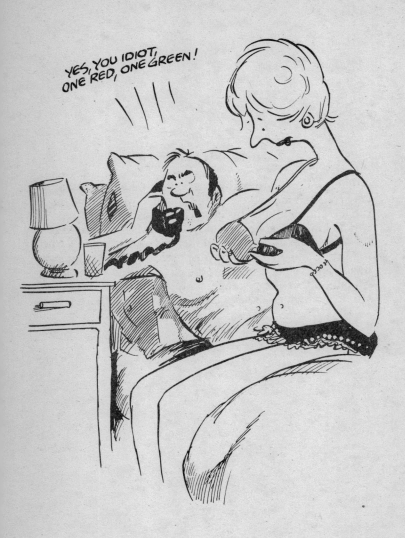

A TICKLISH SITUATION

A lady in Le Havre was just about to take delivery of an eagerly awaited parcel from the postman when he snatched it back and held it to his ear. There was no mistaking – it was ticking. Despite the lady's protests the resourceful postman immediately alerted the emergency services who, in turn, called out the bomb disposal squad. When she was finally able to get a word in, the embarrassed householder explained that the package contained a battery-operated vibrator which must have inexplicably switched itself on.

KEEP IT UP

We did not really need the World Health Authority to tell us, but the official advice on how to live to a ripe old age is: 'Carry on loving'.

Teams of world experts probed the sexy secrets of 5000 lovers before reaching the conclusion that sex is the elixir of life. Actually, a lot of amateurs have known it for years.

Spokesman Dr Marsden Wagner said, 'Sex is of far more value to your health than jogging or dieting. The sexually active definitely live longer and enjoy better health than those who abstain. An uncomplicated sexual relationship is good for the heart, the circulation and general well-being.' Just what the doctor ordered.

HEAVY PETTING

Single Animal Lovers was a dating service opened in California for people to meet each other – and make sure their pets were compatible too. One couple took their goldfish on their first date. Another pair introduced their parrots to make sure they got along all right. And at last report there was a brunette waiting for the right man to sweep her off her feet – along with three dogs, two cats, a budgie, a parrot, doves, chickens, a flock of geese, a horse, wild peacocks and a shoal of fish.

FRAMED

A postman could not resist making passes at girls who wore glasses. But unfortunately they all looked down their noses at him. Undeterred, he settled for the next best thing – their specs. Over a two-year period he snatched thirty-eight pairs of glasses from astonished girls he fancied. When he eventually appeared in court charged with robbery, a psychiatrist predicted that it would take five years' treatment to see him right.

THE CASHIER WITH CHARISMA

Tough-talking bank robber Paul Hawes thrust a gun at the cashier and snarled at her to hand over the money. But something unexpected happened as the pretty girl was filling his bag with £89,000 in Watertown, Nebraska. Hawes fell head over heels in love with her. He dashed out dewy-eyed with the cash – and promptly rang her to apologise. Encouraged by her friendliness, the bandit chatted her up – as police traced the call and pounced. Five years.

HELLO SOLDIER

Every week for eight years after she left school, Marseilles shopgirl Jocelyne Versois-Marchienne sat down and wrote letters to one hundred and forty sailor penfriends. One day they stopped abruptly – Jocelyne announced she had fallen in love with a soldier.

TICKLED

It is an odd fact but true, that bearded ladies are seldom short of a mate. When it comes to sexiness there are men who swear they win by a whisker.

Professional bearded ladies, once familiar in travelling freak shows, are a rarity in Britain. A few still appear with European circuses, but Germany, strangely, has remained the world stronghold of the bearded lady. One of the most famous, Barbara Urileria, had to fight off prospective lovers wherever she appeared.

A seventeenth-century Belgian bearded lady, Helene Antonia, who sported a set of whiskers down to her navel, tickled all sorts of fellows. One of her contemporaries observed, 'The number of men who love her is legion.'

BLOOMING BORES

Hope at last for those quiet, unassuming types who nurse their beer in the corner at parties – suddenly they are in great demand.

Californian Joe Troise launched an introduction agency called Dull Dates for guys who are the life and death of the party. Already there are more than five hundred members, many of them from – yes, you guessed it – Britain.

Joe claims that girls shy away from laugh-a-minute bottom-slappers. Deep down they really love solid, dependable types. Dull men who enrolled were issued with cards entitling the bearer to be uninteresting without penalty or prejudice.

A POINTED GESTURE

Student Miguel Mavallos of Santiago, Chile, accidentally poked his finger in his sweetheart's eye. Overcome with remorse he whipped out a penknife and chopped off the offending finger to apologise. Luckily they haven't yet bumped heads.

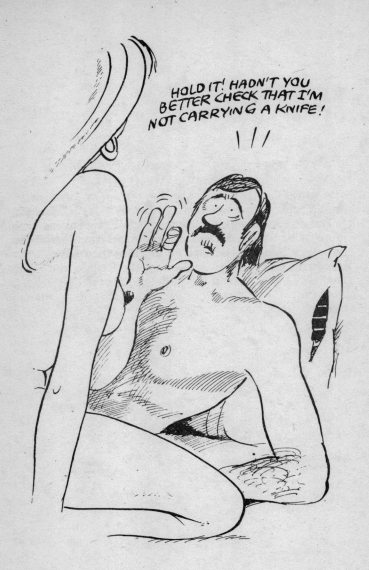

GOOD CONDITION, ONE LADY OWNER

The world's biggest marriage market opens for business once a year in the tiny Indian village of Saurath.

The only commodity on sale is prospective husbands – thousands of them. Bargain basement starts around £200, but pricier models can fetch up to £12,000 apiece.

You have to get there early, though, because more than 100,000 women turn up for the week-long sale. At the end close on two thousand marriages are arranged after hours of heavy haggling.

THE BASHFUL BANDIT

A conceited thief thought he cut quite a macho figure when he was out on his hold-ups. But he had his ego dented when he burst into a Nottingham filling station with a stocking over his head. The lady cashier collapsed in a fit of helpless laughter because he looked so idiotic. The bashful bandit fled, leaving the garage takings untouched.

A BUNCH OF ROSYS

Blessed with a memory like a sieve, two-timing Romeo Janos Istvan should have known better. On Mondays, Wednesdays and Fridays he slept at home with his wife. Tuesdays and Thursdays were nights of passion with girlfriend Number One, while weekends were spent curled up with girlfriend Number Two.

But his memory was so bad that he kept getting their names mixed up. So to avoid a slip-up he made them all change their name to Rosy. The absent-minded motorcyclist managed to muddle through for four years, roaring from one woman to another. It became even more confusing when each Rosy bore him a son. To avoid confusion he called each baby Stefan.

Then one day Janos' life was no longer a bunch of Rosys. Rosey III was cleaning his motorbike when she discovered his three addresses and the birthdays of his sons written on a list in his saddlebag – in case he forgot them.

She rang her opposite numbers and the three got together. Janos' wife divorced him and Rosys I and II sued for maintenance. Janos, 39, said, 'I should have remembered to take that list out of my saddlebag.'

SCREEN LOVER

Between the big picture at a Los Angeles cinema there was a short experimental film entitled 'What Do You Think of My Face?' It was a thirty-year-old bachelor's desperate way of trying to find a mate.

It cost him $1200 to have his face and phone number spread across the screen. Evidently some women thought a lot of his face. He received a thousand phone calls from female film buffs.

BOING?

In the best traditions of tempestuous Continental affairs, French lover Paul Cadet had a blazing row with his girlfriend and tossed her from the fourth-storey window of his Paris apartment. The girl, blessed with the same native passions, bounced off a shop awning and landed nimbly on her feet. Without any loss of momentum she then raced back up four flights of stairs and promptly laid him out with a wine bottle.

THE MULTIPLE HERNIA MAN

Stonemason John Browning had a chip on his shoulder each time a girlfriend threw him over. Eventually he found the only way to bury the memory for good was in the cemetery. John chiselled away his frustration by carving six-foot stone statues of his old flames and hauling them single-handed into Rhode Island cemetery at night and erecting them among the graves.

BOXING CLEVER

At a time when an Englishman might have shaken hands and said 'cheerio', French lover Fernand Gentil went right over the top when his girlfriend jilted him. He threatened to kill himself and have the body sent round.

Unfortunately she was marrying someone else at the time, and relatives worried that the wedding might be disrupted. The bride-to-be laughed and went ahead.

At the reception an unexpected present was laid out among the gifts – a six-foot box bearing the inscription: With the Compliments of the Late Fernand Gentil.

The bride refused to touch it, but her new husband stepped forward and smashed it open. Inside there was a human skeleton. Of course it was not Fernand. When police tracked him down he confessed he had stolen it from a medical school. Six months.

WHAT'S UP, DOC?

Wealthy American doctor Edwin Sandy enjoyed the company of beautiful women – until a girlfriend jilted him. He then embarked on a bizarre plan to take his revenge on all the women he knew.

He spent £100,000 building a luxury booby-trapped house of horrors and then sent out invitations to as many women as he could think of to lure them to the weirdest house-warming on record.

Crowds of unsuspecting guests rolled up at the floodlit mansion looking forward to a lavish party. They were not disappointed.

In the entrance hall hidden air hoses blasted their skirts high over their heads. Staircases straightened out, sending screaming girls sliding headlong to land at the feet of arriving guests.

Sandy's voice boomed through loudspeakers intoning the punishments suffered by famous women who were unfaithful.

Trick chairs collapsed when sat upon and tables fell apart under the weight of a plate. Outside, the luxury swimming pool offered cool relief – until bathers discovered the crocodile lurking in the depths. Sandy, meanwhile, had vanished completely in the mayhem.

HONEST JEAN

Wealthy French heiress Marie Geuard fell head over heels in love with farm labourer Jean Bayen. Everything looked rosy until Jean gave her the cold shoulder and confessed his love for another girl.

Marie, seething with jealousy, paid to have him kidnapped. But even when a gang of toughs brought him to his ex-girlfriend bound and gagged he still refused to go steady with her again.

Marie promptly locked him up and spent the next six weeks whipping and torturing him. Maybe he enjoyed it because Jean still admitted he fancied her rival more.

Finally Marie gave up and in exasperation killed him, burned his body and kept the ashes in a vase. Her rich parents managed to hush up the outrage for thirty years. Marie passed the time talking to the vase until the truth came out on her deathbed in 1806. Even then she was still begging Jean to go steady.

SORRY, I'LL READ THAT AGAIN

There may have been snow on the roof but there was fire in the cellar: eighty-five-year-old Sicilian Evaristo Bertone flew into a rage of blind jealousy when he found a love letter addressed to his wife Adriana.

The vintage Romeo, beside himself with fury at this infidelity, picked up a knife and stabbed his partner in the shoulder. Then he discovered that he had, in fact, written the letter himself half a century earlier. Adriana said, 'His eyesight is poor these days so I forgave him.'

HIT SQUAD

Men in Chile who cheated on their women got a cool reception from a gang of tough girl vigilantes.

The wild women – all karate experts – beat up men discovered in compromising situations or those suspected of assaulting their wives.

Police at Antofagusta did not take reports seriously at first. But they were forced to investigate when more and more men were found wandering the streets, dazed, half naked and covered in bruises.

'The women seemed determined to take revenge on cheating husbands and boyfriends,' a detective said.

After each attack the all-girl gang rang the local paper to give the victim's name and details of what they had done to him. Before hanging up one anonymous caller warned, 'We are determined to show that women here are no longer to be abused.'

SNAP HAPPY

New York male nurse Broughton Wilson could not stand the sight of his wife's mother. He trained his pet cairn terrier to bite her ankles whenever he saw her and rewarded the animal with a toffee every time it scored a hit. Wilson was fined £150 for assaulting his mother-in-law.

THE COOLEST RECEPTION

When health-club masseuse Jane Wells married, the guard of honour at her Canadian wedding wore nothing but towels.

SECONDS OUT

Margaret Cox's marriage suffered a body blow when her husband David, a keen boxing fan, insisted that they spar for a couple of rounds on their wedding night. The bout continued every night for three weeks until Margaret went home to mother. David bought a punchball.

FASTEST TIME BY A HUSBAND-TO-BE

They say that in times of extreme danger, when death beckons, a man's life flashes before him. It happened to Spanish waiter Armando Verez.

He rolled up for his wedding to find his lovely bride-to-be waiting for him – flanked by eight fiancées he had jilted in the preceding four years. All the irate girls brandished cast-iron saucepans and were clearly thirsting for justice. Armando fled and hammered on the door of a nearby police station to plead for sanctuary. The wedding was cancelled.

THE UNINVITED GUEST

As one door closes another opens. Lita Anzano of Asuncion, Paraguay, found a mission in life when her marriage broke up. She gate-crashed wedding receptions to give embarrassed newlyweds unsolicited sex advice. 'My marriage failed because I was too shy to enjoy it,' Lita lectured blushing couples.

MARRIED IN A FLASH

The couple stood nervously at the altar for their wedding listening to the vicar ask the congregation if anyone objected to them getting married.

Before he could finish the question a sudden thunderclap boomed and an almighty flash erupted between the girl's legs.

It was not Divine Intervention. A freak bolt of lightning had struck the church roof, travelled down a metal ladder from the belfry, and run along a power cable concealed beneath the red carpet on which the couple were standing.

Minutes before the service the vicar had advised the bride to stand comfortably to avoid fainting with the tension of the day. She took his advice and without realising it put one foot on each side of the power cable.

The dramatic flash of lightning at her feet plunged the church into darkness and the service had to continue by candlelight.

THE VANISHING VICAR

Anxious bride Mandy Gould was left waiting at the church – by the vicar. Shopgirl Mandy, nineteen, was left in the lurch by a red-faced Revd. Wilf Harris who completely forgot about her wedding in Birmingham to sweetheart Joe Macken.

The bride sat outside the church gates in her limousine for forty-five minutes while guests and police hunted frantically for the vicar. Another cleric eventually stepped in to save the day.

DOWN IN THE DUMPS

Everyone admired the presents at Jane Kay's wedding, but before the bride had time to unpack them properly they vanished. Binmen carted off the lot to the local tip.

Jane and husband George had left them stacked in cartons in a yard behind their new home while they decorated. The couple combed the council dump at Flamborough, Yorks, but there was no trace of the £250 worth of gifts which included cutlery, crockery, glasses, pans, scales – even a lawnmower.

Jane said, 'What made it more annoying was that people usually have trouble persuading binmen to take extra rubbish that isn't in the bin.'

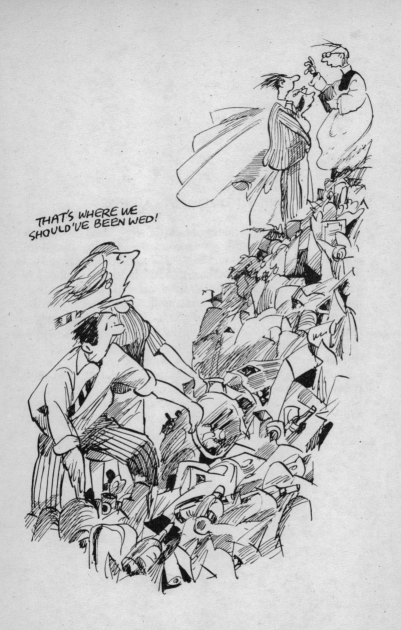

THE WEDDING STAMPEDE

In 1865 the tough pioneers of Seattle were lonely. Most of them were single until businessman Asa Mercer offered to alleviate their condition by placing an advertisement in the Seattle *Puget Sound Herald*. For $300 he would undertake to supply wives from New England. Armed with five hundred firm orders he set out and despite a 7,000 mile journey by land and sea managed to persuade many young girls to return with him. When the shipload of prospective brides docked, the crew had to fight a pitched battle to prevent the local men abducting them.

Back in Seattle the men had cleaned up the town and themselves, and within a week the first wedding took place. Soon every one of the girls was married and even Asa Mercer found himself a wife as his commission on the deal.

THE LOST CHORD

Anna Zucconi could not stand the sound of her husband playing the accordion. She banned Emilio from practising at home and he joined a local band in Milan.

He loved playing with them so much that when he died he left his money to the band. Anna went berserk with rage when the will was read. She smashed the accordion to pieces – and inside found £25,000 and a note: 'To my dear wife Anna – in memory of the days when you were more patient with me.'

FOREARMED IS FOREWARNED

Genetic researchers in America came up with a handy yardstick for measuring happy marriages. Couples whose forearms are roughly the same length from elbow to the tips of their middle fingers are more likely to have trouble-free relationships, they claim. Short-lived affairs, experts discovered, were common among long-armed men and short-armed women. All right, everyone roll their sleeves up.

BURIED TREASURE

Jean Thorton gave up hope of ever recovering the engagement ring she lost – until husband Albert dug it up in their garden fifteen years later. The couple, from Tolworth, Surrey, discovered it just in time to celebrate their silver-wedding anniversary.

HERBERT FINDS HIS VOCATION

Humble bookkeeper Herbert Muller was afraid to tell his wife that his firm had gone bust. He pretended outwardly nothing had changed but secretly advertised for work in a magazine: 'Gentleman will make housecalls to satisfy even hard-to-please ladies'.

After a nervous start, Herbert became a sensation among the wealthy women in his home town of Dusseldorf. The unsuspecting Mrs Muller became worried about Herbert's regular exhaustion, and went to complain to his boss that he was being overworked – only to find the building boarded up.

Back home she searched through his pockets for some explanation and to her amazement found, not paperclips, but a detailed list of his clients and their specialised sexual requirements. The last news was that the couple were trying for a reconciliation.

HOUSE-PROUD

New York newlyweds Richard and Mindy Galbraith looked at the empty plot and wondered how long it would take to build their dream home. Just 6 hours, 55 minutes and 23 seconds later they were relaxing in the living-room cracking a bottle of champagne.

They watched their home grow as two hundred and fifty builders, carpenters and plumbers descended on the site. Building inspectors with stopwatches looked on as the world's fastest house took shape. As soon as the last lick of paint was brushed the happy couple toasted the achievement – then went out to mow the lawn.

PREACHER COX

Preacher Roger Cox felt that there was just one thing standing between him and one hundred per cent devotion to the Lord – sex.

So preacher Cox, a thirty-five-year-old unemployed lorry driver knelt in prayer with his wife in the kitchen of their North Wales council house, and solemnly cut off his penis with a scalpel.

The couple swotted up how to perform the operation in medical text books borrowed from the library.

Mr Cox, a father of eight, said, 'I am happier now than I have been all my life.'

His attractive wife Elizabeth who travelled with him preaching from a double-decker bus, added, 'I support my husband.'

GETTING IT WRITE

Harassed husband Hector Jackman of Cleveland, Ohio, was granted a divorce because of his wife's enthusiasm for writing novels. She invited local tradesmen who called at the house to share 'sex experiences' to provide material for her books.

PLEASURE FLIGHT

A lowdown Peeping Tom snooped on Anne Dawson as she sunbathed in the privacy of her back garden. Nothing would make the sex snooper go away – he was circling in a plane over her sunbed in Grange-over-Sands. The pilot buzzed her for nearly an hour until Anne decided to do some spying of her own. She took his aircraft number and reported him to the Civil Aviation Authority.

SECOND THOUGHTS

Former nun Isadora Colson, 29, found the vows of marriage harder to keep than those of the convent. Her marriage to husband George was annulled when the London Divorce Court heard that she could not bring herself to break her convent pledge of chastity – even after the wedding.

THE BOTTOM LINE

Harassed typists were urged to give office Romeos a taste of their own medicine by equal-rights counsellors.

The National Council for Civil Liberties advised them: if a male colleague pinches your bottom or grabs you – grab him back. If he puts up nude girlie calendars in the office – fight back and pin up pictures of naked men.

A survey of staff in one Liverpool office block revealed that more than a quarter of the one hundred and sixty staff had suffered sexual harassment and more than twenty-eight per cent of the victims were men.

NEIGH, LASS

When animal lover Bill Benn saved an old grey mare from the glue factory his wife Flo was angry about the attention he lavished on the nag.

In the end she ordered, 'Make up your mind – her or me.' Bill thought for a minute and opted for Trigger. And he and Flo, from Yorkshire, never exchanged another word for twenty years.

THE MOST SADLY MISSED PARTYGOERS

Benjamin Weiss and his wife Belle were such a big attraction at parties that he was granted a divorce on the strength of it. An Illinois court heard that Belle, after only two drinks, would strip off. Embarrassed Benjamin had to wrestle with her at eight parties to get her home.

THE COST OF LOVING

Inflation became too much for Wilhelm Stille. The two hundred cigarettes and a bottle of schnapps his wife charged him whenever they made love was too pricy at three times a week. A Stuttgart court agreed and granted him a divorce.

BLOW ME

Libyan Abdul Muni, 37, loved his brother's trumpet so much that he swopped his wife for it. 'It had such a beautiful tone,' he explained. 'I'll never get another like it. Women are just like grains of sand in the desert.'

SILENT PARTNERS

Fred Manley and his wife did not speak to each other for twenty-five years – even when their tempers reached breaking point. Once during a silent row Ted, an ex-London bus driver, grabbed his partner round the throat until her face went blue. But they still did not speak to each other.

Yet amazingly during all those years of suffering in silence the odd couple managed to have three children. They have since divorced.

RUMBLE IN THE JUNGLE

Raven-haired Latin beauty Yvonne Galette had a figure that caught the eye of men drinking at the bar in the gold-prospecting town of Tumbayo, Bolivia. But whenever a randy boozer left arm-in-arm with her he was never seen again.

Finally local police solved the mystery – Yvonne, 29, fed her cast-off lovers to the crocs. She was caught in the act, carrying the remains of one boyfriend to bury him in a swamp outside her village.

Police dug the site over and discovered hundreds of human bones. More than twenty European prospectors were never seen again after a night of love with Yvonne.

THE WEAKER SEX?

Typist Olivia Butterworth broke one of her fingernails when she was using the office typewriter. In a blazing rage she picked up the heavy machine and hurled it through the window. It landed on a passing car in the street below.

An Australian court ordered hot-tempered Olivia to pay the driver for damaging his vehicle.

HIS AND HERS

Eugene Schneider of Carteret, New Jersey, did not want to share his property with his wife. But the divorce-court judge insisted that everything must be divided equally. Eugene took him at his word – and cut their £40,000 home down the middle with a chain saw.

DANGER BEHIND THE BOX

When it came to watching TV George Smith of Ilford, Essex was quite unchivalrous.

He always insisted on watching in the dark which did not make life easy for his wife Pat who had the problem of groping round the house trying to tidy up.

She asked George to put the light on. When he refused point blank there was a violent row. It ended when he was stabbed in the stomach with a kitchen knife. He got over it. But viewing was never the same again.

THE LAST GASP

Despite amassing a million-dollar fortune, Philadelphia businessman Samuel Brett never felt he could spent it the way he liked. He loved fine cigars but his wife banned them from the house.

When he died in 1960 Samuel bequeathed every cent of his money to his wife – provided she smoked five cigars a day.

DAWN CHORUS

A husband in Lyons, France, infuriated his wife by hogging the bathroom so long every morning that she hardly had time to use it. When she could stand no more he opened the curtains one morning and was confronted with the sight of more than twenty housewives waving banners and placards protesting at his daily marathon. The wife had hired the demonstrators to teach him a lesson.

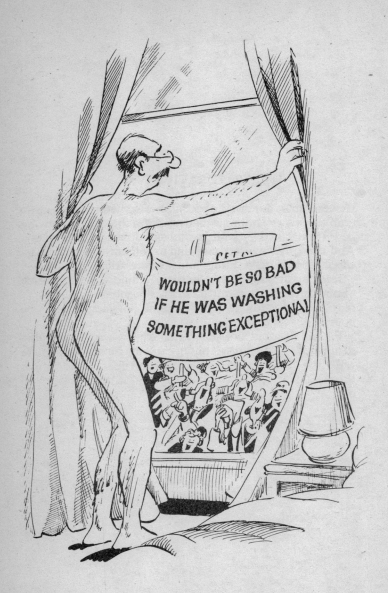

THE MOST PATIENT LOVER

If ever a man deserved a medal it was Dieter Mayer, who grabbed his clothes and made a lightning dive under the bed when his lover's husband came home unexpectedly. And there he shivered – waiting to roll out when the coast was clear and make his escape into the Austrian night.

It was a long wait. The husband, almost twice the size of diminutive Dieter, stayed in the bedroom watching TV, reading and smoking – for a mind-boggling thirty-nine hours.

Finally he went out. Dieter, shivering and barely able to move, dragged himself out just in time for the husband to walk in looking for his keys. He picked up the unfortunate Romeo and gave him two black eyes and knocked his teeth out.

All the stories in *Bill Tidy's Little Rude Book* are true, but the names of some couples have been changed to spare their blushes – or give them the chance to make the same mistake again.